Betelguese, a trip through hell

De Esque, Jean Louis

Contents

WHEN I AM GONE 7

BETELGUESE, A TRIP THROUGH HELL

BY

De Esque, Jean Louis

WHEN I AM GONE

WHAT good is Fame when I am dead and gone,
When in immarcescible regions
My temple rots and soul doth storm and mourn
As bones of mine adorn an early grave ?
Who'll hear and know that I worked hard and long,
That twin sighs and tears storm'd me by legions,
My life, a sunless one—bleak and forlorn.
No ray of light whilst I in thralldom slave ?

What good is Fame when I am dead and gone,
When in fenowed abyss', stark and cold,
I wend my solemn footsteps and atone,
Whilst Fame my brow doth crown with its renown?
Who'll know that heart and soul bled on and on,
That storm-swept aches and woes were mine untold,
My life a waste, from which there stole a moan,
No Aureole whilst I in sorrow drown?

What good is Fame when I am dead and gone,
When far and wide my praise is heard and sung,
And busts and marble-heads my deeds unfurl
To multitudes that knew me not in flesh ?
Not when I'm gone care I for Renown's dawn,
Now, whilst I labour at Fame's lowest rung,
Let me reap dame Approval's brightest pearl

And sip its olpe as I my battles thresh.

CARESSED by crystal dews and light
Beyond the realm of scale and fin,
Incarian Thought flits Fancy wings
To hazards where a crimson urn
Makes scarlet this eternal height
Of sunless suns and reigning sin,—
Flame-decked this plain of warring kings
Where poisoned fumes and beacons burn!
And thro' the hyoids, huge and red,
Past portals black and guidons bright
To onyx lees and opal sands,
The Cyclopean vaults of dwale,
And cavern'd shapes that Typhon bled,
Greet each wand'ring spectre's sight;
Where pixies dance on wind-blown strands,
Lurke gyte incubi in a hall.
Here, then, reigns gyving, batter'd Doom!
Where shadows vague and coffined light,
Spit broths from splinter'd wracks and dome
Where viscid mists and vulpine cries
Rise from the moat of dungeoned gloom
And rasp the stationed walls of night
Until sequesteréd skulls and bones
Are made to hear the moaning sighs
That some mad Titan, rayed in gold,
Wrests from Damnation's siffling tomb.
And labyrinths of Horror's Home,
'Mid vapours green and aisles unsunned,
Provoke each cursing mattoid's fold
Until the night is changed to noon
By cowled magicians on a dome.

Then wizardry, strange, unsummed,
Reveals each varlet, Figgum's might:
A hemless rabble from the South
That some wild Trojan flayed and curs'd,
Skirr thro the Cauldrons broken lane
And wing for implex strands and light,
There, where tapers flare on Hell's mouth
This clan damns each giant Soldan first,
And Medeas in this vast plain,
Who blink at yon dysodile lamps,
Slap thenars and each bifurcous
As javels drink from scyphus' bright.
Blood-curdling monsters on a rope
That sate upon the damn'd one's camps
As hell-winds gleam most glorious—
Each Vandal's music day or night!
Vain! vain! Each isle of hidden Hope!
Alas! Alas! Each olpe of Remorse!
Each vaulted soul and spiral thought,
Swirl in the throes of waters cold;
Where rivers with the venom crawls,
Croak bat-faced incubi till hoarse.
And succubi that Hecate taught,
Bedecked in byss and spangled gold,
Sing runes unto the dungeoned halls.
Then burning ghauts and crimsoned peaks,
Vomit each, green, abhorrent clouds;
The Temple's drum sounds tomb and death
To those that came for unsung trust,
And pyres that smoulderéd for three weeks
Spit wenches blood thro addling crowds
And filch each leering vyper's breath,—
Vile japes that dam all struck with dust!

Erelong unholy fugitives roam
'Mid imbosk caves and moaning dales
To piercing screes of purple gloom,
Where gurgling sighs and rasping moans,--
Each bloody vampyre's home cf loam
As life-tides drip to scarlet vales,—
Unshadowed haunts of darkling Doom !
Add terror to the rasping groans
That roaring surfs of rubic blood
Fling to each afrite's acrid crypt.
And mildewed skulls and ashen boner
That lie before each pillaréd mount,
Speak tidings of a leprous flood.
And where giants carcants flare and sit,
The battle-crests and surging foams
That toss each swoll'n Cauldron's Count
As pyramidal realms unsunned
Glare at the stricken, tamper'd souls,
Stark wenches seek blind seers of lust
And curse each monster's hairless head.
Where fungus-fagots gleam unstunned
As witches dig unfathomed holes
And bury Helms in powderéd dust,
Sleep mourners of the newly dead
Until rayed Aureoles bright, flare,
And sparkle like Asian stars.
Hyperaspists of tempted night,
And yawning caverns cold and bleak,
Forsake the crown of addling Care ;
Whilst afrites in bright jeweled cars,
Lured by the phosphorescent light,
Scale an immarcescible peak.
When giant uncus' of the damn'd

Betelguese, a trip through hell

Shake Palsy's wand of brooding Fear,
And Hecate spins her daughters round
The whirling halls of spastic gloom ;
When afreets prance on blister'd sand
As blood-shot jazels deck each peer,
Each empire froths a raving hound
That storms each zone of purple doom,
And scarlet foam and hiss of oils,—
Abhorrent signs of yawning hell!
'Mid roaring winds and echoes loud
As beaches ring with Torture's hold,
Dim shapes writhe in a cauldron's coils
While canceréd ghouls sound Circe's bell ;
Where hideous screes stem the crowd,
Faffling gawks gleam like burnished gold.

A gangrel imp that Satan flayed,
Shrieks deeds of sin that man-wrecks wrought
Ere gyving Death each culprit smote ;
Where straggling moonbeams cleft a dome,
A Prince in splendor stands arrayed
And rants his spleen unto a ghaut,
Where mongrel whelps their sorrows wrote
In channels with a harlot's bone.

A kingdom vast with jasper light
Greet jejune souls within this shoal,
Where witches lure each helot's eye,
Each gyving hoodlum, seer and sage.
In blazing tankards gleams a sight
As o'er their heads giant rocks roll,
Of skinless nudes that gasp and die
As poisoned lizards vent their rage.

Then vile squats blast the eerie air!
Glozing gnomes of pond'rous built,
Peer at plagues that goddard's hold ;
Writhe vermin in each ghoul-king's olpe,—
Blind death within a secret lair!
A varlet who his wine hath spilt
As Scorpions smote him treblefold,
Is thrown into a stagnant sea
By Lordly Helm of bad repute,
Whose visage, curl'd in ughly mien,
Vext at each leper's font of spleen,
Invokes a hairless witch to scan
The shambling hordes that boon refute,
Who lifts her unguis, long and lean,
To curse each vyper's bloody dream,
Each mongrel and forsaken man.
Then quivers that cippus' hurl'd
As tempted vaults are splinter'd wide;
And fearful fancies cleave the night
When reeking gores pierce hollows black,
Smite vandals that in sleep are curl'd:
And naiads that the vapours hide
In shadows vague—Unholy light!
(Spectres to each soul on a wrack)
Dank caverns of each vaulted soul
With spiral thoughts of feveréd haste,
'Mid the throb of murderous life
In haunted zones of vandals gyte,
Squirm at the pulse of this blind shoal
Where blood-veinéd dreams and acrid waste
Cut thro' the senses like a knife
And bid Icarian Thought to sit
Below a bleak, untower'd home,

Betelguese, a trip through hell

Where fagots that the skelp hath stunned—
Plunderers of unfathomed night!
Glare thro' black shadows vague with forms
Convulsed with cries that pierce each dome
As impeached gumps seek plains unsunned,
(Satellites to mounted Light!)
Teem in the wind-strewn crest of thorns
A phantom that a charnel urn
Spewed from its lap and canceréd fold,—
Trophies of grim Destiny's crypt!
A burning pyre, whose deadly breath
Stir sighs of men as cesspools burn
A harlot strewn with virgin gold
That some malignant, stol'n script,
Condemn'd to witches' fateful death,
Spells reigning doom to one and all.

Where jarbling gumps ride hydras green,
And utter sharp, a curdling curse,
And wingless zimbs that storm each dell,
Glare at each shatter'd dome and wall
That speak of prowling apes in dream,
Of dragons drawing Horror's hearse
When bloody lanes of soulless hell
Bathed monstrous this eternal land.

When Soldans clasp dank Vellum old,
And carcants shine like scarlet foam,
With hiss of snakes and burning oils
As dirges sway both imps and damn'd,
A beacon's light that cleft Doom's fold,
Peers at the Cyclopean home
Of furnace-heat and writhing coils

Of immewed depths as cyphers red
Proclaim each gyving monster's deed.
And woful runes rake this giant gloom,
Phantastic coals lurk in the dust,
Blind whelps lie in an onyx bed
And ponder words as thumb-screws bleed
(Unto the music of king Doom)
Each gangrel villains heart of lust

Beyond the halls of numberéd dead
Where lambent lights and crystal dews
Invoke the ghouls to guard each tomb
That vandals of the sobbing night,
When hell-winds stir the queréd dead,
And thunder shook the mourner's pews,
Giant cavalcades of marshalléd Doom
March thro the phosphorescent light
Unto the headland of the West,
Where pageantries of warriors bold
Scyle crafty sins and purple lusts
Until the peaks and portals bright,
Where buried kings are tombed at rest,
Sweat odours dank with Torpor's cold;
Infernal paeons shake the busts
Of idols planted in the light.
And, ere immewed gyres froth black mists
Unto all ghauts and splinter'd domes
That cypher signs of dungeoned dell,
A turgid dawn arrays this vale,
Each dysodile scavenger sits
On a tomb and fondles gray bones ;
An eyeless toad croaks from a well.
Then cosmic force forsakes each dale :

'Mis Cyclopean pulse of hell
Giant cauldrons vomit vapours green
And skirr thro' bristling lanes and halls :
Whilst beacons die and shrood each soul,
Dank tears drop on a fatal bell,
Wrought by a Titan's sombre queen,
Where graven vypers soop the walls
With blood from maidens scourged as, toll.
Sentinel silence then holds gloom!
Vile squats curse roaring pools inflame,
A swarthy gump leers at the damn'd,
A sultry storm invades each realm.
Reared in incondite depths of doom
As shadows spell each sinner's name,
A Necromancer mounts a stand
That storms and sleet struck with their helm,
And smites the weird elements.
A cesspool stunn'd with offal's stench,

And ulexite—Each mattoid's curse !
Set in twin ridges black and red,
Obtest the foam-sprayed battlements
To count the blood-drops on a bench
That the coals of Tartarus nurse—
Disastrous, imbosked Torture's bed!
Make viscous this grim philster's hold.

Saffron Teocalli in the West,
Whose spiréd domes hold priceless stones,
And censers' fumes lull sighs and moans
As barriers dank, flee their fold,
Betrayed by crystals on a crest
That ride this kingdom's batter'd gnomes,

A fitful syrinx stills all groans
As chasms roar with devils' glee.
Then fancies greet each goblin's eye,
Each donga's depth and mount unsunned:
A quire's rune, in onyx dress,
And black-linkt harps with eyes that see
Each blood-set jazel in a sky,
Where heights eternal reign unstunned,
Pierce sylvan airs that wizards bless.
Come from sequeseréd shoals of hell
Blithe pixies and lithe naiads fair
That revel till the ev'ning skies
Grow lustrous as Arcadian noon.
Then witches in an implex dell,
With stranggling robes and burnished hair,
Flee thro Autumnal shades and dyes,
While quickly from the sandaled gloom,
That struggles at the pillaréd light,
Provoked by turbid drops of blood,
She gleams upon a tower'd home
That gyving hands, of crafty imps,
Reared for the Vandals of the night,
Where seething pores froth devils' flood,
And dusky shales leak scarlet foam,
Or lightly lifts her feet and skimps
Unto a rubic, boweréd vale,
To list unto a clanging bell
That spells these signs to startled wrecks,—
Titan's satellites, Hell and Circe!
The end of her who sought a dale
Below a weird, dungeoned well,
That coffins sunken battle-decks
And a phantasmagoric hearse.

Betelguese, a trip through hell

To muse in gorce's dank and bleak
Mid shatter'd mounts that devil's split!
To mourn in plasmic Temple's fold
With gyving sod no King can shirk!
A spangléd pomp of Death's gray peak
Where owls and lizards blink and sit
As curdling cries of monsters cold
Pierce hollows deep until they irk,
Each surf-thrown afrite's eclipsed dome.
And cursing clans that felt the heat
That dwale obscured in shadows vague,
Clash thro' the broken forest boughs
Until each ronyon's stuck in loam.
There, then, bivouacs a unco Cheat,
Whose limbs were struck with pains of ague,
Who lifts his sightless eyes and sows
The seeds of Thaumaturgist's arts.
Then shakes his fist above all necks
(Whenas the dirges pierce the gloom)
And sheds his addling tears of woe.
Perturbéd at sights of flashing darts
That dragons hurl amongst soul-wrecks,
He smites a staff upon a tomb
Where phosphorescent torches glow,
And mouths his words at earless owls,
Past ribboned dusk and pillaréd woe,
Where sonless maids their sorrows heal,
And mixes purple mists with light,
Both moaning airs and cringing howls,
The swirling skelp that heavens show,
And changes this vast plane of weal,
This kingdom's tomb of rasping night

To elfin cheer as dances bloom,
And speeds his flight from Terror's urn,
Past jasper lanes where moonstones glow,
And turns his eyes at writhing Hell,
Upon the spectral haunts of Doom,
Where fiends in hissing Cesspoles burn
'Mid howls of pain from vassals flow
That rake each skull-blown vale and dell.
Where syrt sucks jargling javels mad,
And carcants cast a luring light
From mildewed screes and mounts that scyle
Veiled augueries of battling Hell,
A charnel shard assails the damn'd
Thro' vapours green and siffling night;
Monastic caverns rasp each isle;
A poisoned skink croaks from a well.
And mournfnl wraiths sob hard and loud,
A smotheréd sigh proclaims more woe,
The lounging imps grasp tomes of old
And rant therefrom each damn'd one's name.
And horrors, snarling at each crowd,
Assail each kingdom with its show:
A noctivagous dragon bold,
Hastes thro' the aisles of death and shame
And haunts the cajons of the dead,
There fungus-tapers gleam like gold
Before a ghoul-king's jeweled throne:
There, too, upon a Temple's arch,
Bivouacs a witch who scans the bed
Of buried kings and queens struck cold
And lifts her voice to splinter'd dome
To stem the brooding Djinnee march,
And with the dusk that meteors split,

She tries the figgum of her lust,
And throws her voice at portals dark,
Past burning pyres, where moaning airs
Call the help of Conjury's script;
And, ere cyphers burn in the dust
The names of new souls in this ark,
The ghosts of the dead prance in pairs.
This is the sphere of Dust and Tomb !
Where Trojans struck with palsied Death
As Satan smote each cavern's fold,
And whistling heat swirl'd Circe around
The coffined slabs of Aeæa's womb,
When kingdoms fought with rasping breath
As stellar domes grew black and cold,
Auric oriflammes storm'd the mount
As bristling lances smote giant hordes;
Then gorey devils fought with lust
As vulpine cries smote each jinn's ear,
Black Dragons swore beneath their breath
And murdered all rebellious Lords;
Strong hands that knew each axe's trust,
Escutcheons that all princes fear,
Hurl'd swift destruction and black death.
Where Titans storm'd a Monarch's throne,
There sleeps a Ruler carved in stone;
Where vultures guard a serpent's home,
A quarteréd warrior tells its tale.
Perturbéd at dews that drip from dome
As wattling apes their horrors groan,
The witch forsakes each glozing gnome,
Affrighted at this gurgling vale.

On crimson mounts where hydras peer—

Affronting devils in the gloom !
Unsypheréd regions wrapped in light
That hide dank vapours of each tomb,
Lurk throaty imps throughout the year
Who sing their runes as lepers soom;
Red-embered gnomes within this night
Where scarlet dyes bathe Torture's womb !
And Djinnee gasps add to the sight
That dragon-worms bred in this surge,
Build temples for queen Sorrow's home;
And pageantries of Typhon's bloom—
Immarcescible sklayres of night !
And shadows bleak, that sins do purge
A show for Satan on this throne !
Invoke the Cauldron's spraying gloom
To newer deeds of hell-lashed lust;
Tho' dusky wizards rake the skies.
(Eternal hounds that all beguile)
Unstable dreams lure Fancy fane
Below this star's unfathomed dust,
Where shatter'd domes list to the sighs
Of skinless wenches on an isle,
Where nymphs call her Christian name.
Where purple mists like poppies bloom
Dank dulse within green rivers cold!
A flayed and sobbing maid doth lie;
Eternal curse of bedlam night
Speak of sepulchral haunts of Doom;
Unnumberéd skulls their woes have told
To studded domes and opaque sky
Beneath the Arching vales of light.
Alight with fires red and green
That show the coffers of each tomb,

Betelguese, a trip through hell

Jarbling vandals rake the night-coals,
Shales and husks; and, ere reigning night
Provokes each harlot's fitful dream
To cleave the casements of king Doom
And reach the swoll'n, acrid shoals,
Where stationed Mounts are penciled white
That mark the maw of raging hell,
Till, eyes awake stare at each flame
Unsung and, on boulders that burn,
Peer at two lordly squats in dust
As wenches drink from poisoned well,
'Mid purple sins and naked shame
In Typhon's olpe and churning urn
Of stranded devils, souls and lust.

When earthly homes are tombed in dust,
And Life forsakes geotic shoals;
When midst the tombs of penetence,
When coffins damp, and slimmy clay,
Each Lordly Helm is tossed in trust
To spiral vaults from plasmic holes,
Convolving cyclones spin him hence
As agate torches light his way.
Unmutteréd sighs teem in the air
As structural stars pass him by,
And twisting clouds shape eerie forms
Until he reaches Satan's home.
Unholy visions curse and swear,
Gyte vypers lull each demon's sigh,
Giant Dragons whom no Remorse storms,
Shake fists at opals in a dome.
And Cesspools vext with odours strong
From stifling shard and putrid dung,

'Mid caverns large and Cauldrons deep,
Vile squats in teeming pewter burn;
And shrieking vypers wield a prong
Above a monster, quarter'd hung.
The Tasmanian Devils keep
The sod turn'd in a gyre's urn
That no lost soul can undulate:
Hence seers and sages, tossed in sin,
Rant rubies to each reigning king,
Each glowing pyre is fed with oil
By afreets reared on bottled hate;
Infernal tapers light this Inn
As poisoned vapours to us cling;
Re-embered beacons on this soil
Flare spastic shadows to each tomb

In vain we sigh for fleeing grace
Within the pale of turbid dyes !
In vain we look for hope, sweet rest,
Within this crypt of whistling Doom !
When in monastic nights of haze
The battlements retard giant sighs;
When marshalléd mists from out the
West Cloak ramparts black with ughly light,
A rubic Soldan rakes each ghaut,
Each sleeping vandal, imp and soul.
No astral eyes laugh from these skies,
No nightingales sing in the night;
A dungeoned curse that villains wrought
Rasp each eternal vault and shoal.
Then one-eyed mongrels split the dyes
Of roaring winds and raging storms,
Dim shapes flee to the haunts of gore,—

Each Cyclopean Dragon's goal!
And groaning cries from maidens fair
Is heard by spectral, gangrel forms,—
The writhing thin is flayed some more !
Its secret sins,—Black deeds of Soul—
Is scourged as copper-burnished hair
Hangs from her alabaster head,
Both feet and arms are screwed till black—
A sign that Hell reigns on, unstunned.
Then incense swung by priestesses,
Salute the newly, plunder'd dead,
The bloody sight upon the wrack,
Where cringing groans once rose unsummed,
Is cover'd by the murderess.

Where restless hawks and chainless ghouls
Blink bleary orbs at dust and stone;
And glozing night-gnomes love the sight
That geysers toss upon their crest,
Feal afrites bathe in a pool
And wash each harlot's bloody bone.
Scorpions on serai's height
Peer at each forge's raging breast,
Whilst faffling gumps aud hairless seers
Stretch shanks and arms and yawn till hoarse,
And vapours green and beacons red,
Feared coming Dawn, and fled in haste;
The bulwarks that each hoodlum fears,
Sink in a cajon's livid course;
The winds and storms are silent, dead,
As barriers red bathe the waste.
What of the sight when Horrors swirl,
When oceans ring with Terror's roll?

What of the galley-decks and wrecks
That felt the force of angry Hell?
When kingdoms fought each warring Earl,
The incubi cursed each lost soul;
When vandals broke the idols' necks,
Giant battle-axes smote each dell.
And, then came there galvanic gloom !
An acrid oath and savage howl,
Hurl'd at an idol's austere ghoul
By grizzled rogue and mocking gnome,
Perturbéd as vandals shine and bloom
In robes of pearl and tazzled cowl,
Throw Hecate's spawn into a pool
Who stung them with a poisoned bone.
This wanton witch of evil fame,
Vamped with both hatred, murder, lust,
Speeds cycles of the Future's curse
And damns each goblin, skink and knave.
Then pyres and ghauts flare once again,
The halls are swept with burning dust,
Six Dragons bear the dead one's hearse
Unto the newly, opened grave.

Ere the quaking Dawn shakes its crown
To tower'd peaks and hyoids red
That hide blind fathoms of this sea,
An opal light arrays each plain;
Each naiad rumps on velvet down;
A bat-shapped Buzzard makes its bed;
A red-tongued Gecko storms each lee.
Then apes and adders writhe with pain
As Cauldrons vomit oils that burn;
Mid churning storms of stinging sleet,

Betelguese, a trip through hell

Vial haunts of gore spill their quest
And murder with unholy lust,
Wilst fagots, beacons, torches, turn
Hell's Pompeian shoals to heat;
And viscid mists rise in the West—
Dank treasures of Damnation's dust !
In search of silence, sleep and rest.

When in a vale we lie and dream
Of sanded beach and laughing skies,
When Fancy lifts her wings and soars
To agate strands and ocean's breast,
A gangrel soul begins to scream
Black tokens of prevailing sighs
As furnace-ovens sweat giant pores.
And other things perturb each crypt,
Each vulture's brood and figent owls:
A belching mountain in the South
Hurls boulders thro the fearful night:
A demon-quire rants from script,
Led by staccato raspings, howls ;
A meteor vaults a Cauldron's mouth ;
A sombre maid doth long for light.
Bleak wintry winds engulf us all—
Hosannah! cry the fretful mobs ;
White-heated storms assail all heads—
Triumphal paeons shake the air!
Unnumberéd gawks roam thro' each hail-
Where Typhon sits, a maiden sobs!
Conscience stabs our nightly beds,
Remorse leers daily at dame Care.

A Donga, deep with squirming gnats

And acrid coils,—a hole of Death!
And runnels thick with arid dung,
Flow past a Temple's swoll'n arch,
Where warring tribes of hungry cats
Fish for green lizards filched of breath ;
A palace-dome where runes are sung
As Satan views his squadron's march,
Flare twin mineral lights of blue
That lure each legion foul of home.
Swarm Trojans right and left with sword ;
Skirr gloppened worriers thro the night ;
Roar puteals that toads eschew;
Hiss brown snakes to each toothless gnome,
Affrighted at the raving horde
That crash thro' leprous filth and light—
Disastrous sights of men gone mad!
And pyramidal wall of rock
Are battle-grounds for waging lust:
A clashing lance spun vypers round
The gyrus rind where helots clad
Each Thaumaturgist in a frock,
The sign of which spake added trust
Unto each ghoul-king's able hound.
Crafty Lords of militant mien,
Led vanquished to the slaughter-pen;
Thumb-screws and bastinados work
Both Devils' pomp and Soldans' joy;
And tantrums coarse in cesspools teem
As women sob for dying men :
The wracks that djinnee fear and shirk,
Are Torture's friend—A Monster's toy!

The rayless styes that guard the bones

Betelguese, a trip through hell

Of fall'n kings and grizzled hordes,
The mildewed screes that hold the skulls
Of shambling spectres, wraiths, and souls,
Now waft the spiréd, rasping tones
Of risen helots, princes, lords ;
And all up-rising mists from hulls
That stranded on these jejune shoals,
Evaporate when amber lights
Cleave phantom-screens and huddles black
(For this each pixie sings for cheer)
Arcadian sights then hold sway:
Each corporal gump loves the sights—
The hidden past (an endless track)
Reviews each garneréd Greek and year,
Each warrior bold and lassie gay.

Sanious lights beyond the height,
Imbosked dysodile vaults of dwale
As ulexite flare in the rocks
Where implex aisles lead to gyte doom,
Lure illaqueate Thought to flight,
And at a Cyon, chained in stall.
Whom mad Medeas shore of locks,
Chase Fancy's wings where hazards bloom.
Here herculean dwangs of gold,
Clasped in talons of Circe's son,
Pry portals of Teocalli as,
When hyoids blaze like sea-linkt skies,
Incondite imps seek grovels cold,
Unfathomed haunts that scyle each sun,
We see above the lees green grass
Where pixies laugh with dancing eyes,—
King Wonder's sight that holds each heart!

Above the rind of Ursa's wake,
Past shadows vague and sunless suns,
Giant visions of the cancelléd past
Rise from the void and play their part.
Demeter floats around a lake;
Where waters with a naiad runs,
Hector's shot by Archilles' dart ;
Where Orestes stabs his mother,
Agamemnon sleeps on in cold ;
Aegisthus robs a queen of all;
Andromache sobs tears of woe.
And Clytaemenestra's lover,
Like Menelous, is strong and bold :
Aeneas on a burning wall
Carries Anchises from the show.
Then vulgar scenes stare at each soul,
Hair-raising visions greet each eye;
Priam's son is dragged round ancient Troy,
Tied fast to a chariot's tail ;
Andromeda's doomed as Death's toll ;
Patroclus dies with a deep sigh.
Phyrrhus sacks Troy with a devilish joy ;
Hecuba's nineteen sons now wail As
Mycenae and Tiryns are burn'd:
The Scaean Gate is storm'd by Peers!
Archæans and Phrygians bold
Have fought with Hatred's biting lust.
Telemachus whom the Fates have spurn'd
Finds Ulysses in twenty years;
Thessalian Soldans in gold,
Like Daedalus, slept on in dust
As Penlope winged for distant zones.
Then Syran airs held each ear:

Betelguese, a trip through hell

Bright carvels glowed with rubic wine,
Giant cyphers flared each Lordling's name
Within the haunts of dungeoned domes,
Where jazels peer the eyes of Fear,
And owls with a scorpion dine—
Twin Monarch's play the dice's game.

When beacons urticate each eye,
Noctivagous ghouls haste to stroke
Each goblin shank of hoary sage.
Then pomp of gloom breaks into bloom,
The Temple's arch cracks as we sigh,
A clashing sound above that spoke
Blind wrath unto each Wizard's rage,
Revealed the chasm of stark Doom.
Unto the peaks and gables black,
Syrian airs like Orpheus
Lull sequesteréd afrites to sleep,
A witch smites her high biforous
A symbol of king Typhon's wrack!
Where crystal lamps shine most glorious,
Twin legions lie in cajons bleak,—
Tokens of Hell invidious !
Then fades the burnished light on high;
Magicians stave their heads in dust,
The vermin feed on reeking bones,
Each gnome sobs to a green-horn'd toad.
And monarchs of this dungeoned sky
Untomb each son in sacred trust
As vypers sound their rasping tones,
Farewell the ancient Greek's abode!
Then spectres of the tower'd night,
(Vultures of the sun, moon and stars)

And bezzling parasites of dawn,
Haunt ichnolite of mourners cold;
Then purple sins bloom in the light
As vypers drive queens in bright cars;
Where dragons root the blistere'd lawn,
There reigns a curdling monster bold.
To scour these lanes of strobic gloom—
Infernal doom by mongrels' wrought!
To pace these aisles of whistling heat,
Eternal signs of souls gone wrong!
And when a skelp cleaves siffling doom,
And vapours scyle a greenish ghaut,
Rebellious vandals stamp their feet
As rulling Cyons wield hell's prong.
Then domes and walls sweat savage rage,
Each gangrel gnome is toss'd by fear,
The tombs provoke each inmate's keep
To curse the horrid atmosphere,
Where ghouls their battle-axes wage,
Froth devils' pomp throughout the year ;
Where lizards o'er tath do creep,
Bivouacs a horney-fisted seer.

To groves of wind-swept ulmus' bear,
And siffling mists beyond a bell
That hide veiled shadows of a peak
Above the stationed domes of red,
Augueries of a marching pair,—
Twin demons of unconqueréd Hell !
Spell visions that the soffins leak
That felt the besom of the dead,
Just as the Twilight's scarlet urn
Is seen from heights unfathomed, strong.

Betelguese, a trip through hell

There runnels of green waters cold,
Toss lepers from their murky breast;
There venom-oils and tapers burn
To light the way of souls gone wrong,—
Blood-stainéd each idol's crown of gold
Where battle-wrecks seek figent rest!

To the distant porphyry mount
Where agate torches shine most bright,
And syrinx's float music's charm
O'er the jargling herds of tombed,
A joggling javel begins to count,
With bleary eyes of grayish light,
The rubies on each idol's arm,
And whisper words unto the tombed.
Now to a churning gyre's pool
We haste to see a weird show,
Where Lordly Helms in vials squirm,
Each mongrel scoundrel's olpe of wine!
A Morgan gambles with a ghoul,
A Belmont writhes with sizzling woe,
A Rockefeller leads each worm,
Another's known as T. F. Ryan.
The browless whelp of oily fame
Is made to dig the burning soil,
The sheckles of a Pierpont king,
Secures no prestige in this Inn.
The gambling ghost whose middle name
Is Fortune", spins within the swirl
Of waters cold and oceans' ring,
Condemned, forsaken for his sin.
On earth they plunder'd, robbed and stole
From month to month and year to year;

There Franchise-stealers cracked with leers
As Plebeians stung, groaned with might.
Now one and all damn'd on this shoal
Yuck addling brains and shriek with fear,
Now all shrink at Hell's laughing seers
As Remorse storms the ughly night.
Here Pat McCarrens filch no vote,
A Grady eats no mellow pea,
A Murphy owns no City Hall,
No Jeromes skew at dices' song.
On Vellum gray their sins are wrote
To murmurs of each sullen lee,
Racked with the wand of death and pall,
They blast their heads as souls gone wrong.
No presidential timber's found
Within these caverns, pools or dung;
No two-faced B's or bloated T's,
Lie to laymen, vassals, hordes.
Here politicians hear the sound
Of ballots that their hearts have wrung,
Of burning pyres and blister'd lees
That scorch these one-time kings and lords.
Here Conventions hold our eyes
As Dragons smite a gravel dome.
The kings of Finance, skinn'd and shorn,
Are list'ners in these halls of gloom.
Their deeds are read, they heave giant sighs,
Thumb-screws and wracks rake skin and bone,
In cajons bleak, each corpse forlorn,
Is sunk as trophies of king Doom.
No Depews sell their patron's love,
No faffling Platts guard treasures strong,
No Parkers, Roots,—The crafty things!

Betelguese, a trip through hell

Betray a country's hope and trust.
No palm is brought them by a dove,
No minions shant their praise in song,
The poisoned zimbs add to the stings
Of conscience lost and raging lust.
Each one-time king of earthly fold
Is skinn'd alive then cooked in oil ;
Some frazzled Astor dames and fools
Now eat their claws and chew a bone.
A monarch known as Leopold,
Writhes in a cavern's squeezing coil;
Here man-born helms are but the tools
Of Satan and each prowling gnome.
Their toes are screwed and eyes are bored,
Their ears are shorn and lips are split,
Each head is cracked, all tongues are cut,
By vypers red and bloody ghouls.
Affrighted as the dames are gored,
Each Sybarite his teeth doth grit,
The huddled pirates in a hut,
Shriek help unto the roaring pools.
And moaning airs their sorrows tell
That some unfathomed force hath bred.
Night-hawks rasp sins of women, men,
Who sold their honour, soul and name.
And tower'd screes that pierce giant hell
Are treasure-houses for the dead:
Each rich man writhes within a den,
Society dames proclaim their shame.
And offal, shard and putrid dung,
Is by affluent daughters born.
When in the ribboned' mists above
A beacon flares and torches burn,

A Soldan from green earth is hung ;
His heartless queen is cursed, forsworn,
Their souls house neither hope nor love
Within Damnation's burning urn.
Repress'd with hate and unspent rage
As charnel howls clash in each hall,
Each gyving hydra rends the air
With curses, hawps as rambling souls,
Lured by a grizzled warrior sage,
Storm moats before each bristling wall
And die as imps are bade to swear—
Infernal trophies of these shoals !
Immingled dreams their senses storm
As Westward shadows cloak each lee;
Where censers blaze they drag their limbs,
These cursed, forsaken whelps of hell!
Their ghastly sins on vellum's sworn,
Attested, sealed, they bend each knee !
Where devils rant blood-curdling hymns,
A raving wench drowns in a well.
Unto the coals of feveréd pyres
That glare like carcants red and white ;
And glowing rubies in the dust
That lure each man-born skink and whelp,
The spastic cries and moaning sighs
Attest to Typhon's weird dight,—
And Satan's ichor of green lust,
Provokes the lashing heat and skelp.

Within the cathedral vaults of gloom,
The gorgeous pomp of the flayed,
In banded gold and marble flesh,
Speak of auguries to the damn'd,

Betelguese, a trip through hell

Till, when censers' lights flare and bloom,
And shapes of men are laid arrayed
In gomes of steel, we tred the mesh
And grandeur of a conjured stand,
Where coral wreathes each hussy's brow,
Whose broken arms portray hell's lust,
Of whistling winzes, syrt and domes
That gleaming broths in anger wrought,
Mid hiss of snakes and oils. So now,
When plunderéd tombs betray their trust
And vandals screech at roving gnomes,
All raise a voice and curse each ghaut.

Beyond the ring and roll of hell—
And spiral lofts of quartz and gold—
We skirr upon the crutch of haste
And cleave the abyss, cold and bleak.
There jejune fossils lie to tell
Of pleiocene days' garneréd fold;
Gray bones that pierce this weird waste
Lie mounted on a torrid peak;
Principalities of the past,
Lie scatter'd in the mildewed dust;
Serai's built in ages gone,
Now crumble at a sound, a voice.
And Boulders that the Djinnee cast
As Vengeance swirl'd the heated dust,
Now rock as devils rasp a son,
And vampyres dance round and round.
And where a dim, unstudded dome
Leak odours strong and palsied light—
Twins of the Gloom ! as some mad soul
Assails Typhon's battling walls,

Betelguese, a trip through hell

A glowing fire of this home
Of deadly dews and poisoned night,
Bathes monstrous this untower'd shoal.
Convulsed with fear as aisles and halls
Roar like giant cauldrons mad for gore,
Icarian gumps and devils bold,
Assault each marshalléd mount and scree.
Then spectacles greet us again
Upon this shadowed, foreign shore:
A pondrous dwang of virgin gold,
Is filched from altars that we see,
Just as the tomb-sweats pour like rain.
And distant ghauts where jazels burn,—
(A burning tomb where hissing oils
Drip on a flayed and bottled wench
That some abhorrent spawn of death
Filched from the wrack of Terror's urn
As stagnent breath unwinds its coils)
Spout uncoped shard unto a bench
Where sights of men-wrecks gasp for breath,
Whilst quickly from a bowelless whelp
Drop ghastly stones of scarlet hue
That brazen imps hurl thro the air
At sobbing wraiths and furrowed souls,
Wrought by a fiend and conjured skelp
As men and women hold a pew
Within a turgid, acrid lair,—
Infernal aisles of yawning shoals !

T'ward cyphers bright and terrible,
Where Doom sits poised as Satan yawns,—
Each Vulture's home and arid shoal!
We hurl a curse and damn the hordes

That call each monster horrible.
Then craftily he moves his pawns
(Whenas a moan escapes each soul)
As bleary sons of noble lords
Sway twin censers' fumes in silence,
Until in myrtle groves we see
A blazing arch where agate eyes
Doth peer malignly from a crypt
Thro' turbid phials of violence,—
A scene of impish sorcery!
Where, in furbished chambers there lies
As vypers write on evil script
The ghastly deeds that sinners wrought—
A glow-worm's fagot that arrays
Dim shapes of souls of men that were.
And cyphers nights of doomes to be,
Till flaring pyres and yon red ghaut—
So monstrous bright that some one prays
And Vizy's carvel starts to stir,
Shape abhorrent signs on each lee.

Into the dusky, coals we peer,
And musing at the luring flames,
We watch each isle of crystal green.
Anear the billows swirl with rage,
'Mid lashing waves that cope king Fear
To strands and sands where elfin games
Make rich each midnight's fleecy dream
That some Mad wand'ring, goblin sage,
Provoked from coffers of each brain,
Gleam in each tossing breast of foam,
Or shines from purple decks and domes
A ruddy carcant huge and large;

Or, when sea-linkt clouds, garbed in rain,
And behemoths sink to briny home,
A star that shines from foreign zones
Guide carvels old and Satan's barge
O'er blue profounds of the deep,
And gladden souls of men; yet, stunned,
Tho' trembling, to a roaring mouth,
A horn'd magician locked in death,
On whom two hectic harlots peep,
Sinks in abyssal depths unsummed,
Whilst him he fought hastes to the South,—
A hoary fiend of rasping breath !

And now we watch a maiden flee,
Past seas and ice-mounts oriflammed
With crystal diamonds red and bright,
Where Persephone hath breathed a jem,
And frozen jazels that we see,
Alife with lusts of curst and damn'd,
Tho windblown, thro' the moonless night,
She wanders with her anadem
On golden hair; nor doth she haste
When scarlet eyes peer thro the snow,
But cavernéd mouths of grottoes black,
And storm-swept flight of dragons bold,
She passes as she treads the waste,
Off to the haunts of ghoullish show,
Where fires writhe and whispers track
Her wake unto the peaks of cold,
Above whose tower'd dome she sees
The tombs of father, mother, all;
Ay, now weeps she as the head-stones
Letter large, her unburied kin.

Now with her trembling arms and knees,
And back against the slimmy wall,
She vents her tears and choking moans,
A daughter cursed within this Inn.
And witches long for ease, so,
Erelong they peer at waters green
That pour in forges dank and cold,
Whence glare the eyes of Hell in lust
As Cyclops stem the pyre's glow,
'Mid haunts of sin and purple sheen
Of shales and husks of monsters told
As vultures to both scale and dust.
Then wing they for the western strands
Of bowveréd vales and lulling dells,
Where silence holds the winds at bay,
And myrtles stir the sylvan air. ,
There tow'rs and the russet sands
Make fine the tunes of ringing bells
That echo to the skies of gray,
Where phosphorescent lanterns flare.
And twilights of the lofty aisles,
Thro silver mists and streaks of blood,
Crucifixion looms cold and white;
Oaths of prurient blasphemy
Echo to the sequesteréd isles;
An ivory pyx that rides the flood
On which fantasms spin their light,
Curse each soul's eternal enemy.
Within a pool where writhing coils
Shape cyphers bold and gorey thought,—
Two shadowed sklayres of Doom and Set!
The foam-dreams of the newly dead Ascend.
To hazards that the oils

Eschewed, haste dryades that were taught
To dance. And, whilst all souls forget
The chasms deep and oriflammed,
The spastic lights of a green room,
Dim torches show the jeweled tombs
Wherein are hid the studded crowns
Of Eastern queens; or, when high-bred
Dames pick from Death's unbroken womb
The coral wreaths and poppy blooms,
Two priestesses in scarlet gowns
Curse loudly as the royal dead
Are strewn with palmy leaves and dyes.
And crimsons adders on the hulls,
Search for toadstools smeared with blood,
And livid lamps where vypers spoon,
As some bad harlot shrieks and cries
Her Nature's sins unto three skulls,
A shameless gnome bathes in hell's flood
The thighs he filched from a gray tomb.

Drawn by the whispers from the wind,
'Mid glories of the hollowed night,
To storm-swept vales and mounts we haste,
And, in monastic halls we see,
Above a greenish gyrus rind,
The flick'ring flames of a light,
Beneath whose subtle, shadowed waste
Squat men and women that would flee
The ghastly words from Vellum told,
Who pluck their eyes and pull their hair,—
Beneath their feet there writhes a worm!
As bludgeons smite a leering soul.
And when a wench that Satan sold

Betelguese, a trip through hell

To some old seer, whose head is bare,
And oily snakes in cauldrons squirm,
All blast the sight and curse this shoal,—
Infernal land of Sin and Doom!
Eternal moans and sighs we hear;
A swarthy demon laughs with glee.
Then, thickly from a ghastly hole
The turbid dyes of blood doth bloom
From minxes bold, crouched with giant fear,
Provoke a sage who could not see,
With feelings for her impeached soul.

Low arches of a charnel house,
Above whose dome two demons sit,
That guard the lamps of fateful red,
Veiled whispers from a maiden's soul
Cleave skyward until they arrouse
A savage hound of hell with script
That holds her body's deeds. A-bed,
He peers thro' shades unto her shoal,
Then at his tome where sins are wrote
Of wifes that sold their names in lust,
Or men that worshipped naught but gold.
And, when stillness holds troubled sway,
A baneful imp that Conscience smote,
Rasps names of those bowed in the dust:
And, when thus their sins are foretold,
As kinsmen strike their beasts and pray,
A livid gasp permeates the air,
A curdling curse assails the night.
And squats, whose scarlet venom crawls
To lantern's-glow that tell the guilt
Of battling demons as they swear,

Malignly dumb below each light
That scyle the bloody walls and halls,
The life-ebb from a wench is spilt.
The phosphorescent fungus-lights
Are traitors' lamps that sorrows hide;
The foam-sprayed beaches that we see,
Are treasure-houses for the damn'd.
From year to year infernal nights
Rasp shoals a thousand furlongs wide;
In ev'ry zone, each distant lee,
Holds ghastly sights of burning sand.
The headlands that we reach by day,
About whose shore the dragons roam;
And mildewed vaults of gatheréd bone,
Where eyeless skulls and ape-shanks lie
As moaning winds reel to and sway
From gorey pools and tower'd dome,
A goggling wraith and shambling gnome
Doth forage for each fleeing sigh.

Now Sorrow that the Dooms crown'd King,
Flees from the mouth of pools inflame,
Whilst Lords in robes of scarlet hue,
Add to the damn'd, malignant show;
Pellicles that all eyes did sting
In Vengeance's law that none could tame,
Flees whence two lights of dreaming blue
Cleave dome-thrown shadows dress'd in woe.
A Thaumaturgist, cursed and damn'd,
Raps skulls from which a venom pours,
And shakes his fists where opals burn,
Whence figgum that his hands control
Is charged with life; and on the sand

Two witches sate their thirst in gores,
Flit Fancy's wings unto a urn,
(Within whose tomb there writhes a soul)
And with Courage that Dawn hath bred
In rivers, to whispers of the night,
As wracks are dyed a crimson red,
Feasts upon Doom's abhorrent shape,
That fires bright, toss to each bed,
And flees to realms where shadows light;
Whilst Thought, in horror of the dead,
Wings in mourning veils, dark as crepe,
And feasts on afterglow of Trust,
On cauldrons tossed to crafty Death
That froths dank pomp and guidons bright,
Unto a height, where falt'ring eyes,
Betrayed by crystals numb in dust,
Gasps at the sight with startled breath
As vapours green, war with the light,
Faint as the sunset's golden dyes.
All mounts of bone are tombs of weal,
Each scree, a temple of king Doom;
And runnels that the suns do shun,
Are pools where offal reeks most strong
And thro' the air giant wasps do reel;
On barriers bleak, reptiles soom;
A Vulture that no shard can stun
Gawks at the multitudes gone wrong.
Where waters with the venom crawls
To oriels, where banners float
Beside a dome-thrown surf of blood
Tward letters large, that Hell hath wrought,
Worm-like vapours skirr thro' the halls
And reach a distant, lurid moat,

Where sighs and groans upon a flood
Ascend to heights of a grey ghaut—
Satellites to Destiny's crypt!
And Vespers that the Twilight brought—
More dooms that prayers nor sighs can break—
Leer at each thought to Fancy's flight;
And to the dais whereunder sit
A demon-quire that Circe taught,
Songs that echo to the isles in lake
And valley deep, ravage the night
Until Idols pall at the scene.
And stationed Mounts toward the West
Whose bones portray a ghastly lust;
And skulls that glare at the soulless night,
Point, weeping, where the foam-waves dream:
All battle-wrecks and imps haste forth
Unto the phosphorescent dust
And pyramidal shoals of light.

The poisons that the geysers spit
To apes, where Sin in splendor reigns;
And cavern'd shapes that shadows hide
Behind tapers, where snarling Doom
Glares at Set's tomb, where devils sit,
Make vague signs to the weird flames,
Flit spastic breath to regions wide
And shrood each shrunken soul with gloom.
Where glozing parasites hold sway,
Seck rivers dry reveal the bones
Of ages that the Cyclops slew:
Onyx thrones that the Titans storm'd
Lie in obfuscating decay;
Eyeless skulls that abhorrent gnomes

Wield in hands that reek with the dew
That solemn Death in tombs hath worm'd,
Stare at the scene as willows sigh:
And tapers of the Mount's crown'd witch
(Whenas each carcant fades from view)
Seek shadows that the tombs have cast
Upon the conjured, wind blown sky,
Where Syrian altar-lamps make rich
The palace-domes whereon the dew
Sits like a star and beams upon the vast,
Phantasmagoric glory of Death,
Of godly helms housed in a crypt.
And where a livid beacon flares—
(A rock that some giant storm hath split)
In mourning robes and rasping breath,
Before a grave where devils sit,
A Queen at whom a lizard stares,
Sobs her grief and woe that tears writ
Deep into the phorphyry mount:
This, then, is Deaths home, vale and Tomb!
Where Lancers, made equal with the dust
When revolt storm'd each kingdom's fold,
And clashing wars spun Hecate round
The pungent halls of spastic Doom;
When in each Nation fought king
Lust As siffling vapours gleamed like gold,
Ten legions whom the gods forsook
Wrought havoc on this Cauldron's shore:
Then Dragon-guidons led the march
As battle-axes smote vile Lords;
Stout hears that with king Vengeance shook,
Fought with valour's shield for more gore;
Assaults that rasped each Temple's arch,

Spake conquest o'er shambling hordes.
This tale on ghastly Vellum's writ,
More sypher'd woes the walls proclaim;
Where goblins fondle crumbling bones,
There lies a death-thrown monster cold.
Perturbéd at writings on yon script
As moaning airs gaunt Sorrows name,
Each ape attests in faffling tones—
Flight to the Dragons' haunted fold.
Affrighted at this fearful gaze
As coals blaze like twinkling jewels,
Night-hawks that croak at bat-faced owls
Gledge at each gnome that digged a bone
From some bleak pool, and pierce the haze
Where censers blaze. Unconqueréd ghouls
Who laugh and leer at demon howls,
Make signs unto the hell-lashed foam—
Japes that the damn'd fear in each knell!

Where jargling javels stab a toad,
And mutter swift, as vypers swear;
And spectres that the cauldrons wrought,
Glare at the storm-swept sins that tell
Of monsters that the night-winds rode
When bloody plumes stole to a lair
Beyond the confines of a ghaut.
And spacious halls where vagrants lie—
Vandals to the Dawn, Night and Dusk!
And vulpine labyrinths of hell
Where pirates of a star are thron'd
As dews cloak bones that pierce the sky,
Wowed witches with a gorce's lust
When vales list to a clanging bell

That some encharnel'd hybrid domed,
Sweats cesspools with the pall of fear,
Shrill sounds permeate the barren air,
Each shatter'd light before a well,
Ends its flame in short, spastic gasps.
And stars that burn but once a year,
(Veinéd Aureoles to altars where,
When sins are told unto each knell
As chanting runes are hushed with clasps
Of winds provoked by black-set night,
Peer at the caravans in prayer;
A dirge is sung by magicians;
Each Idol squints eyes at the show,
Whilst goblins curse the eerie sight.
And Betelguese, an evil lair
With infernal, warring legions,
Careens as stars shed tears of woe.

Arcadia, its pleasing name,
An Eden where the damn'd drink wine,
Where rich fetes greet each varlet's eye,
Each gyving hound whom Fates have doomed:
Each scyphus veils a burning flame;
A blood-stone from each dome doth shine
On poisons that in goblets lie,
Bred by sorcerers, cursed and tombed.
Then Terrors, Horrors, reign supreme!
Each vial squat before the spread,
Leer at toads in goblets crossed,
Froth skinks within each feaster's glass,
Wine changed to blood, then acrid green.
A drunken villain who was bled
As drink his convulsed entrails tossed,

Writhes with the cramps upon the grass
And glares at the face of his god,
Whose wrinkled skin, in ghastly wrath,
Provoked at this son in revolt,
Rants his spleen to the slabs of Doom,
From whence gyte monsters with a rod,
That oft gave imps a bloody bath,
Hythe, and before their master halt;
And, then came unhung, battling gloom!
The dome cracked like a clashing star,
All lights were muffled in a shroud,
Wild winds that cought us in their fold,
Dashed wrecks unto a reeking zone.
In Thralldom's grasp we waged giant war,
The storms rasped at each cursing crowd,
From regions far there sprung a cold
That froze each hoodlum stuck in loam.
There, garbed in the wastes of a moat,
Gangrel witches scan the slime to curse
Beneath a dome and shatter'd light,
A sign that all are lost and doomed.
Toward jagged heights black oaths float,
To skies of jasper light, adverse
To Doom's rich fold, prayers reach thro' night
That some malignant monster tombed
In phantom-blankets stark and bold.
All mountain-chasms growl and roar;
Each ocean froths black waves of lust;
King Thunder rasps the trembling night;
Giant lightnings split their fevered hold;
Encharneled guilt hastes to this shore
As hydras squirm along the dust,
Affrighted at this Cauldron's sight.

For we are unsubstantial wrecks
Beyond the pale of scale and fin;
Adventurers tossed by king Time
In region neath supernal skies.
To dungeoned knells where venom specks
The robes of priestesses with sin,
And prowling apes get drunk with wine
We turn each thought to coral eyes
That seas have blurred with coffined night,
And whisper deeds wrought in silence.
A quiver that the tomb-sweat bore
When walls were split with Typhon's ire;
And monstrous shapes that carved the light
As dragon-worms brought pestilence
To souls who grovel on this shore,
Proclaim each gyving djinnee sire.
And dryades whom the mists have struck
With ague—A Sceptre of Despair!
(Sklayres to the night, and suns unstunned)
Dank dulse, where templed vaults of man,
Coarse-grained, who gambled with king
Luck, Mid pulse of life below the air,
Shake at the throb of this unsummed Sphere,
where haunted thoughts and dreams scan
Athward at a untower'd home,
Where vitals that the glow-worm lit
Friends to the Doom! as sorrowed soui,
Repress'd with rage, knelt down and prayed,
Rise from the hollowed void a moan
As sins upon papyrus, writ
In vyper's blood—Jems in this shoal
Confess'd by men whom friends have flayed,
Teem in the wind-swept, shatter'd strands

Blind batter'd keels that know no rest
'Mid surge of moans that tombs have spilt.
Upon the air that Doom hath wrung,
Beyond the fields where numberless hands
Point to the headland of the
West, Lights and vague shadows spell no guilt
Unto the wraiths whom Torpor stung.
And all night-thoughts in this strange sphere
Tred in the skirts of waters cold,
Of hell-winds that the beaches swirl
Dome-high within this shrunken realm;
And crested billows toss giant Fear
Unto each culprit's hidden fold:
The studded roof where flares a pearl,
The charnel vapours o'erwhelm.

In caverns where gyte jinnee lee
Noctivagous lepers in the gloom—
Unhollowed regions wrapped in light
Where groans are drowned by revels coarse
(Seen by a gump throughout the year
Above the strife where horrors soom)
Lurk crafty gnomes who with the night
Rant oaths in voices cracked and hoarse:
Blood-thirsty jinn in essling caves,
Where rubic dyes tinge Torture's dome,
And vypers' whispers pierce the night
As ghouls—whose baneful eyes conspire
With the surge of hell's roaring waves
Rear mounts of bone—Dame Sorrow's home!
As charnel scarn parades in light
Unfathomed crafts rayed in wowed attire.
And dusky mists peer at the show,

Obtest the gloom to further deeds
Of haste, to Horror's added might;
Tho' twilight-witches spill their gloom,
(Betelguese's priestesses of woe)
Abhorrent gawks lure in the reeds
Where shatter'd lights wing sudden flight,
'Mid spun-waves kiss'd by poppy bloom.

Dank dulse, and rushing waters cold;
Eternal signs of shadowed night
Beyond the zephyr-haunted space
Of adequate lees 'neath the sky:
Unfathomed haunts of stark souls bold
That squat on waves of darkest dight,
Malignly mute as foam-waves race
To pyres where men in torture lie.
When thrones are levelled to the dust,
And glories fade in cauldrons tossed,
'Mid waters vaster than the night
In scarlet tombs that rasp grim Death,
Supernal selves, loosed from king Lust
As Dissolution bulwarks crossed,
Conviction of an undreamt might
Assail each mongrel afrite's breath.
Hushed gasps permeate the solemn air
As coral Twilight flaunts its sheen,
And vapours wreath phantastic forms
Till vaulted domes glow like the noon.
Vague dreams plague souls beyond repair,
Phantoms, black demons call their queen,
Skinks and owls whom no conscience storms
Make faces at the leprous moon.
And bleak dungeons dank with odours

Strong, within each encrusted gyre,
'Mid treasure-vaults digged by gray
Age, Affronting witches incense burn;
And howling ghouls gape thro' vapours,
Two siffling vampyres dance on fire,
Each mottled sage a conqueréd page
To him whose hate no Doom can turn,
No bat-faced gnome can stem the blaze:
Hence harlots, ghastly with giant sin,
Chant runes to him in strobic gloom
As figgum's plied before his throne.
Malignly mute, he peers thro' haze;
Infernal paeons shake each Inn,
Blue lights 'twixt opals burn and bloom
In deep-hued haunts of Typhon's home.

In vain we seek an isle of peace
Beyond the pale of siffling Doom!
'Mid stillness vaster than the tomb,
Made equal with the ghouls who lurk
On battlements where witches ease
Their minds as rubic censers fume,
A Fiend bubbles in ruddy bloom
As turgid dyes the night-dwales shirk.
No sunsets crimson this stainéd sea,
No Ev'ntides her plume unfolds;
An opaque light that Silence wrought
Careens thro' space in quest of toll.
Then demons storm each sea and lee,
Abhorrent sights each Cauldron holds,
Dim shapes flit to the distant ghaut
Where Doom sits poised—Each monster's goal
Erelong the air shakes with a roar—

Betelguese, a trip through hell

Forebodings of souls on Death's dome!
Bright cyphers spell the new-damnéd name
In letters gainst a leprous home:
Oaths peel like the hammer of Thor
The screaming thing is flayed to bone
Its sins—an outraged Body's shame
Laid bare as whipcords dye the foam,
Whereon nepheloid imps and night,
Soom on with tidings of a moan,
Of dews, and whisper'd groans and sighs.
And, as vague forms writhe in despair,
A native in phantastic dight Stills
Torture's hold in weazened tone,
Black incense lifts its wand and flies
To haunts where mattoids rave and swear.
Where figent gawks sken at a gnome,
Decked in byssin and beads of gold;
And glozing jinn on a scree's height,
That leer as geysers boil and flow,
Feazing imps on serais dome,
Drink from olpes icy philters cold,
Whilst scarn assails the morning light
And gumps haste to the Dawn's first show,
Then pyres don mystic sklayres agleam,
A faffling fool leads gawks thro' hall
Where fays, in stones of ancient art,
Dance as Scorpions shake with glee:
Infernal pomps spread tawny sheen,
Strange figgum, amid unholy pall,
Pierce Sorrows with its poisoned dart
Whence horrors shake their limbs and flee.
And scenes, profound in Aspect's hue,
Play havoc with eyes of each soul:

Crimson dales (vague tho' they be)
And swards rise from the lurid moat;
Knees bend in Adoration's pew,
Blithe songs of cheer, far and near, roll
Thro' the halls to ebony sea,
Above whose breast twin whispers float
Tremendous signs of dooms to be!
And, ere falt'ring noon wings itself
To shadow peaks and portals bright
That scyle veiled augueries of Hell,
An agate light arrays this sea,
Each glabrous fay sports with an elf,
A one-eyed owl blinks at the light,
A green-horned toad croaks from a well.
Then pageantries fade in the gloom:
'Mid Cyclopean storms unstunned
Dank treasure-houses spill their quest
And march with thunder from far West;
Whilst lightning flashes skirr the noon,
Giant moans ascend from shoals unsunned,
The turf, Tartarus' coals of rest—
Helots to the haunts of Sin's crest—
Whereon jimp jinn ride to hell's mouth,
The silence stir with oaths of might;
Vile dragons roar at a zimb's sting;
A swarthy gump leers at the damn'd:
All soom to mountains of the South
Where sultry winds war with the light,
And zanies' voices rise to sing,
Hosannah to the idol's stand,
Where azure-censers' fumes enhance
The pomps, adverse to Sorrow's home.
Figent hydras squat on each throne,

Mute souls peer at the altar's flame
As phantom images do dance
In honour of this Hybrid's zone,
Bred in this gorce by some strange gnome,
Sib to him who plays Satan's game.

A Cesspool vext with leprous stench
And oils—A sign that spells a curse!
Visioned with Temples' diamonds bright
In domes as guide to those whose cry
Of fear, sprung from a wench's bench,
Lure all to this strange shore, adverse
To moonlit skies. By the ghaut's light,
(Ten-thousand furlongs wide and high)
The gaud, spun from sorcerers art,
Reveals its part unto each soul—
Imperishable signs of groans
That time nor cyclones can eschew.
No lulling lanes point to a mart,
No tidings good their billows roll;
In fretful haunts where Sorrow moans,
Swarm souls in Penance's rasping pew:
Disastrous sights of Torture's dome!
Red-embered coals that burn their feet
And reeking pools, vile with odours,
Make monstrous this blood-crimson vale.
Where demon-lovers chew a bone
As men and women choak in heat,
And blood-veinéd sights writhe in vapours
Eternal shadows in each gale!

To groves where stiliness sat supreme,
Flee seers in quest of lagging rest:

To regions where giant echos roar,
Haste begotten sons in this lair:
There man-born wrecks lie down and dream
Of sea-winds that foam-billows bless'd,
Of auric realms where censers pour
Violaceous fumes thro the air.
And in the deep-hued depths of gore,
(Blind bowels in Betelguese's hold)
Gyte vandals that a Dragon bore
Sleep with one eye as Midnight rules
These sons of Circe whom pyres adore;
Their thoughts vie with the luring fold,
Each sleepless orb glares like a boar—
Infernal hounds of shambling ghouls!
Porphyry mounts where crystals glare
Twin carcants strung on idols' thighs
Whereon stones, blaze like fire bright,
And moonstones add their silver sheen,
A Circean draught, boiled in the air,
Is poured on cippus where Set lies;
Where vanquished Soldans sleep each night,
A greenish fungus-torch doth gleam.
Giant battles have been fought in hell,
Principalities rot in dust,
The tombs of kings speak of the past
When Incubi reigned with a rod.
Unnumberéd bones adorn each dell—
Where Rulers lie there stands a bust;
Blood-stainéd the hands of him whose task
Is blasting varlets like a god.
And when some spirit stalks thro' space
In quest of vaults—Temporal lees!
Treads in the grandeur of dank hell,

Betelguese, a trip through hell

A batter'd shape that shakes its frame,
Spacious regions Courage chase,
Winds drive it to Misery's seas,
Laughs ascend from sequestered well,
Thro shadows vague it hears its shame.
And tomb-thrown groans and sighs we hear
Tho' midnight's near and afrite's sleep:
An Owl, perturbed at some strange sound,
Scares bats in space and wings for domes.
All signs of woe hath flown with fear,
No maidens heave their breasts and weep,
All wrecks of Flesh lie on the ground,
Removed from shoals where Terror moans.
On skulls that some in Death hath left,
Croak toads to lizards in a well
In cajons that the Ancient's digged,
Swim snakes that hiss at burning oils:
And bats and owls that offal cleft,
Proclaim their burdens to a dell,
Whilst crafts that some strange witch hath rigged,
Bring slaves unto this Cesspool's coils.

When carcants gleam like scarlet foam,
And hiss of pyres froth at each light
In dongas vext as jazels flare
From splinter'd tombs of Kings in dust,
A straggling mist that cleft Hell's dome,
Peers at the gloom and strobic sight
Of charnel shard as vypers blare
Wrathfully at each Monarch's bust.
And doleful dirges rake the gloom,
A whisper'd sin sobs at the wrecks;
Graven imps clasp papyrus old

And rant each Body's deeds of shame.
Come from a dank and sunken womb
All stranded ghouls on keels and decks
Where Cyclops fought as Vellum told
In cyphers bright, sprung from each flame,
Make hideous eyes at the night.
And terrors that Tartarus bred
Assail each kingdom treblefold:
A gangrel clan that someone flayed,
Skirr thro' the dungeoned halls in flight
And seek the caverns of the dead.
Where tapers gleam like virgin gold
The tombs of dead queens are arrayed:
There, too, a witch unfurls her cowl
And scans the shambling hordes to curse,
And with the light that cyclones split,
She juggles secrets of her lust,
And hurls her voice at Néphele's owl,
Past portals dark, where harlots nurse
Their skinless limbs that Torture bit,
And stamps her feet into the dust
As, into olpes she pours a tear:
And, musing at the clouds of gloom,
She wrinkles face and lifts her hands
To mutter words unto the night,
Whereon a ghoul-king hath writ Fear,
And changes gloom to purple bloom,
The shoals to opal-sanded strands
That reach, past wrecks to crystal light,
Where mossy vales with poppies bloom,
And hastes her flight from Terror's urn,
To onyx seas where agates glow,
And feats her eyes on woes of hell,

Betelguese, a trip through hell

Upon the foam-dreams of king Doom,
Where monsters in red cauldrons burn,
'Mid shrieks that from their vitals flow
With airs that rasp each bone-strewn dell.
And sea-linkt skies of charnel black—
A savage dome! streaked scarlet red,
Where maids for demon lovers mourn ;
And caskets spew a dusky foam
That quench the thirst of yon lone wrack
That holds the sultry, naked dead,
Who caught the eyes of waves forlorn,
Now bathed in blood in Hecate's home.

There garnet wrought and purple lights
Shine thro poisoned vials of age
On churning pomps of casements old,
Where, when lofty aisles and halls
Ring rich with tenor runes in nights
Made solemn by a hoary sage
With darkling eyes that gleam like gold,
A prowling vandal storms the walls,
Nursed with dank venom broths and oils.
A blood-shot minx hunts for a man;
In stys and broken pyxs she peers
For him who ruined her honour, soul;
A harlot doomed in clinging coils
That now her longings curse and damn,
Squats on a skull and pulls her ears:
Or, just when she finds her life-goal,
A cow'ring cur hid from the sight
Beneath a putrid mount of bone,
And tombs grow dank as rising sun
Makes red each dragon in the West,

She splits his heart and rasps with might,
A curse that rides the surging foam,
A message that this dastard son
Dies longing for a fatal quest—
Surcease of soul and conscience lost !
Then rants she sins unto each tomb
That sweat the lusts of those in dust,
And scarlet foam and hiss of oils
That her black deed to domes hath tossed,
Break into writhing life and bloom
As iron crowns and ceptres rust
Of fall'n monarchs crossed in coils.
Anear, two carcants glare like gold ;
Afar, a ruby's light of red
Straggles thro' the pellictéd mist,
And to its vine wed dell haste I,
To catch the fleeting whispers told
To marble-lamps and head-stones, said,
By demon-husbands as I list,
To hold each mongrel harlot's sigh.
There, then, in tatter'd rags and hair,
Coarse-grained of features once so fine,
She spews her 'evil wrath and rage
Into the wriggling hands and face
Of him who lifts his voice to swear
A curse that stirs the air, whose time
(Tho' to king Satan speeds a page)
Hath come as Vengeance wins the race.
When crimson skies and stellor eyes
Swathed palace domes and turrets strong,
Her lips kiss'd mine, and mine did hers,
Ere evil smote her virgin soul.
And livid lights of bleeding dyes

(Whenas she prods him with her prong)
Make terrible her words so terse
That brands this scoundrel on this shoal.
And mutt'ring quick a ghastly oath
As turgid mists veil shadows vague,
She plucks his lying tongue that stole
Her husband's love and honour old,
And smites him stark and cold tho' loath
It peers to me her demon-ague
That binds her to this perjured soul,
She drinks his gore from carvels cold
And leers with fiendish lips at him,
Now tossed in phosphorescent holes.
And as I list to aspen cries,
Veiled augueries in vapours hie
And spell these tokens to each Inn:
Kingdoms, empires, nations, souls,
Shall miss the haunts of Paradise,
And in Subjection, crumbling, lie.
And when the regions, wrapped in light
By pillared dreams and pomps supreme
As curses stir the charnel air
That hide dank caverns deep and bold,
A battling monster smites the night
As lepers wink their orbs and dream
Of maidens that, the men forswear,
Of templed vaults now stiff in cold.
And when a dim, unholy tomb,
Wreathes odours damp and vapours strong
Heirs of the Doomed ! as savage domes
Drip palsied sweat and carnal howls
Assail the stationed halls of gloom,
Where imps and devils march along

Betelguese, a trip through hell

Beside a monarch's crumbling bones
As witches don their filthy cowls
And rant their sins thro' whistling halls,
Shake women fists at fleeing souls
And wail for batard children dead;
Whilst quickly from the burning dust
Ascends an oath that storms the walls
And rasps the distant mounts and shoals
Until each pyre glows scarlet red,
Each idol leers with wicked lust.
Forth from rubies flare scented fumes
As beacons glare and bubbles hiss
To crimson strands and altars' glow
Of burning oils in carvels deep,
Where; when Torture's bloody dome looms
Cold as shambling shapes of men kiss
Trembling women before the show,
Wraiths point to where their daughters weep.

To lie in vaults and chambers cold
'Mid tombs that ghouls in hatred wrought !
To sleep in dank Subjection's shard
'Mid hanuts of purple sins and shales
A Thirst gyre ! as bleak, untold,
As ever haunted woman sought
For incubi on scented sward
As bleary owls and vulpine wails
Rake stationed nights and seas forlorn,
Until, when star-linkt domes are red,
And Oceans' shells and sands grow white,
Dusky isles and lights—Twins of the Gloom!
Betray each soul cursed and forsworn ;
Or awed, at Twilights' scarlet bed,

Betelguese, a trip through hell

When nightshades blot the conjured light
As javels vomit death and doom,
Dank vapours veil the seaward flight
Of Satellites gray 'gainst the night,
Till, eyes in fear peer at profounds
Unfathomed and, in vales unsunned,
See Cyclops battling in the light,
'Mid scarlet foam and gorey sight
Of bloody domes and hybrid hounds
Of Titan's forges, cold, unstunned.
Oh, vain each sinner's prayer of hope !
Alas, alas, all thoughts of future trust!
The bloody lanes of reigning Doom
Are lasting tombs for souls accurst.
When in a pool we lie and mope
As vaulted temples rot in dust,
Vague shapes and forms ascend to spell
Infernal chasms of black gloom.
When crested waves of billowed sea
Are lashed by winds from foreign shoal,
And foam-set breasts are dashed on high
As silence holds the voiceless air,
Unsavoury dreams haunt each lee
The maw of Hell receives a soul !
A leering fiend blinks at the sky.

Beyond the realm of railing Care,
Caressed by suns and moons most fair,
We fain would hye, all wrecks, and lie
In dusky forests dells and vales;
Beyond the Asian skies of blue,
Where sports an elf, mayhap a hare,
We fain would haste, each soul, and die,

Unfurl all dreams and pinioned sails,
And sleep unmourned in haunts we knew,
Now wracks and domes stare at each soul,
Giant goddards leak a rubic foam;
Blind forges hold Contagion's breath;
A Morgan longs for earthly home. ,
Tis so with hell's eternal shoal
Where skinks eat flesh from wenches' bone;
Tis thus with us purloined by Death,
Infernal doom that spells a moan.
Ten thousand years was Doom crown'd
King; Sporadic prayers each gnarl'd one lisped;
Despotic sway all subjects curs'd
When Hell was new and Earth unborn:
Now souls of man in torture sing,
Each Idol's glyph by damn'd one's kiss'd.
Who then shall say who is the worst,
A vyper's brood or man forsworn?

www.bookjungle.com email: sales@bookjungle.com fax: 630-214-0564 mail: Book Jungle PO Box 2226 Champaign, IL 61825

The Codes Of Hammurabi And Moses
W. W. Davies

QTY

The discovery of the Hammurabi Code is one of the greatest achievements of archaeology, and is of paramount interest, not only to the student of the Bible, but also to all those interested in ancient history...

Religion   ISBN: *1-59462-338-4*   Pages:132
MSRP $12.95

The Theory of Moral Sentiments
Adam Smith

QTY

This work from 1749. contains original theories of conscience amd moral judgment and it is the foundation for systemof morals.

Philosophy   ISBN: *1-59462-777-0*   Pages:536
MSRP $19.95

Jessica's First Prayer
Hesba Stretton

QTY

In a screened and secluded corner of one of the many railway-bridges which span the streets of London there could be seen a few years ago, from five o'clock every morning until half past eight, a tidily set-out coffee-stall, consisting of a trestle and board, upon which stood two large tin cans, with a small fire of charcoal burning under each so as to keep the coffee boiling during the early hours of the morning when the work-people were thronging into the city on their way to their daily toil...

Childrens   ISBN: *1-59462-373-2*   Pages:84
MSRP $9.95

My Life and Work
Henry Ford

QTY

Henry Ford revolutionized the world with his implementation of mass production for the Model T automobile. Gain valuable business insight into his life and work with his own auto-biography... "We have only started on our development of our country we have not as yet, with all our talk of wonderful progress, done more than scratch the surface. The progress has been wonderful enough but..."

Biographies/   ISBN: *1-59462-198-5*   Pages:300
MSRP $21.95

www.bookjungle.com *email: sales@bookjungle.com fax: 630-214-0564 mail: Book Jungle PO Box 2226 Champaign, IL 61825*

The Art of Cross-Examination
Francis Wellman

QTY

I presume it is the experience of every author, after his first book is published upon an important subject, to be almost overwhelmed with a wealth of ideas and illustrations which could readily have been included in his book, and which to his own mind, at least, seem to make a second edition inevitable. Such certainly was the case with me; and when the first edition had reached its sixth impression in five months, I rejoiced to learn that it seemed to my publishers that the book had met with a sufficiently favorable reception to justify a second and considerably enlarged edition. ..

Reference   ISBN: *1-59462-647-2*   **Pages:412**   *MSRP $19.95*

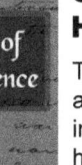

On the Duty of Civil Disobedience
Henry David Thoreau

QTY

Thoreau wrote his famous essay, On the Duty of Civil Disobedience, as a protest against an unjust but popular war and the immoral but popular institution of slave-owning. He did more than write—he declined to pay his taxes, and was hauled off to gaol in consequence. Who can say how much this refusal of his hastened the end of the war and of slavery ?

Law   ISBN: *1-59462-747-9*   **Pages:48**   *MSRP $7.45*

Dream Psychology Psychoanalysis for Beginners
Sigmund Freud

QTY

Sigmund Freud, born Sigismund Schlomo Freud (May 6, 1856 - September 23, 1939), was a Jewish-Austrian neurologist and psychiatrist who co-founded the psychoanalytic school of psychology. Freud is best known for his theories of the unconscious mind, especially involving the mechanism of repression; his redefinition of sexual desire as mobile and directed towards a wide variety of objects; and his therapeutic techniques, especially his understanding of transference in the therapeutic relationship and the presumed value of dreams as sources of insight into unconscious desires.

Psychology   ISBN: *1-59462-905-6*   **Pages:196**   *MSRP $15.45*

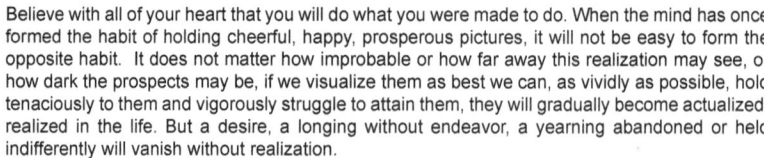

The Miracle of Right Thought
Orison Swett Marden

QTY

Believe with all of your heart that you will do what you were made to do. When the mind has once formed the habit of holding cheerful, happy, prosperous pictures, it will not be easy to form the opposite habit. It does not matter how improbable or how far away this realization may see, or how dark the prospects may be, if we visualize them as best we can, as vividly as possible, hold tenaciously to them and vigorously struggle to attain them, they will gradually become actualized, realized in the life. But a desire, a longing without endeavor, a yearning abandoned or held indifferently will vanish without realization.

Self Help   ISBN: *1-59462-644-8*   **Pages:360**   *MSRP $25.45*

www.bookjungle.com email: sales@bookjungle.com fax: 630-214-0564 mail: Book Jungle PO Box 2226 Champaign, IL 61825

QTY

	Title	ISBN	Price
☐	**The Rosicrucian Cosmo-Conception Mystic Christianity** by *Max Heindel*	ISBN: 1-59462-188-8	$38.95
	The Rosicrucian Cosmo-conception is not dogmatic, neither does it appeal to any other authority than the reason of the student. It is: not controversial, but is: sent forth in the, hope that it may help to clear...		New Age/Religion Pages 646
☐	**Abandonment To Divine Providence** by *Jean-Pierre de Caussade*	ISBN: 1-59462-228-0	$25.95
	"The Rev. Jean Pierre de Caussade was one of the most remarkable spiritual writers of the Society of Jesus in France in the 18th Century. His death took place at Toulouse in 1751. His works have gone through many editions and have been republished...		Inspirational/Religion Pages 400
☐	**Mental Chemistry** by *Charles Haanel*	ISBN: 1-59462-192-6	$23.95
	Mental Chemistry allows the change of material conditions by combining and appropriately utilizing the power of the mind. Much like applied chemistry creates something new and unique out of careful combinations of chemicals the mastery of mental chemistry...		New Age Pages 354
☐	**The Letters of Robert Browning and Elizabeth Barret Barrett 1845-1846 vol II** by *Robert Browning* and *Elizabeth Barrett*	ISBN: 1-59462-193-4	$35.95
			Biographies Pages 596
☐	**Gleanings In Genesis (volume I)** by *Arthur W. Pink*	ISBN: 1-59462-130-6	$27.45
	Appropriately has Genesis been termed "the seed plot of the Bible" for in it we have, in germ form, almost all of the great doctrines which are afterwards fully developed in the books of Scripture which follow...		Religion/Inspirational Pages 420
☐	**The Master Key** by *L. W. de Laurence*	ISBN: 1-59462-001-6	$30.95
	In no branch of human knowledge has there been a more lively increase of the spirit of research during the past few years than in the study of Psychology, Concentration and Mental Discipline. The requests for authentic lessons in Thought Control, Mental Discipline and...		New Age/Business Pages 422
☐	**The Lesser Key Of Solomon Goetia** by *L. W. de Laurence*	ISBN: 1-59462-092-X	$9.95
	This translation of the first book of the "Lernegton" which is now for the first time made accessible to students of Talismanic Magic was done, after careful collation and edition, from numerous Ancient Manuscripts in Hebrew, Latin, and French...		New Age/Occult Pages 92
☐	**Rubaiyat Of Omar Khayyam** by *Edward Fitzgerald*	ISBN: 1-59462-332-5	$13.95
	Edward Fitzgerald, whom the world has already learned, in spite of his own efforts to remain within the shadow of anonymity, to look upon as one of the rarest poets of the century, was born at Bredfield, in Suffolk, on the 31st of March, 1809. He was the third son of John Purcell...		Music Pages 172
☐	**Ancient Law** by *Henry Maine*	ISBN: 1-59462-128-4	$29.95
	The chief object of the following pages is to indicate some of the earliest ideas of mankind, as they are reflected in Ancient Law, and to point out the relation of those ideas to modern thought.		Religion/History Pages 452
☐	**Far-Away Stories** by *William J. Locke*	ISBN: 1-59462-129-2	$19.45
	"Good wine needs no bush, but a collection of mixed vintages does. And this book is just such a collection. Some of the stories I do not want to remain buried for ever in the museum files of dead magazine-numbers an author's not unpardonable vanity..."		Fiction Pages 272
☐	**Life of David Crockett** by *David Crockett*	ISBN: 1-59462-250-7	$27.45
	"Colonel David Crockett was one of the most remarkable men of the times in which he lived. Born in humble life, but gifted with a strong will, an indomitable courage, and unremitting perseverance...		Biographies/New Age Pages 424
☐	**Lip-Reading** by *Edward Nitchie*	ISBN: 1-59462-206-X	$25.95
	Edward B. Nitchie, founder of the New York School for the Hard of Hearing, now the Nitchie School of Lip-Reading, Inc, wrote "LIP-READING Principles and Practice". The development and perfecting of this meritorious work on lip-reading was an undertaking...		How-to Pages 400
☐	**A Handbook of Suggestive Therapeutics, Applied Hypnotism, Psychic Science** by *Henry Munro*	ISBN: 1-59462-214-0	$24.95
			Health/New Age/Health/Self-help Pages 376
☐	**A Doll's House: and Two Other Plays** by *Henrik Ibsen*	ISBN: 1-59462-112-8	$19.95
	Henrik Ibsen created this classic when in revolutionary 1848 Rome. Introducing some striking concepts in playwriting for the realist genre, this play has been studied the world over.		Fiction/Classics/Plays 308
☐	**The Light of Asia** by *sir Edwin Arnold*	ISBN: 1-59462-204-3	$13.95
	In this poetic masterpiece, Edwin Arnold describes the life and teachings of Buddha. The man who was to become known as Buddha to the world was born as Prince Gautama of India but he rejected the worldly riches and abandoned the reigns of power when...		Religion/History/Biographies Pages 170
☐	**The Complete Works of Guy de Maupassant** by *Guy de Maupassant*	ISBN: 1-59462-157-8	$16.95
	"For days and days, nights and nights, I had dreamed of that first kiss which was to consecrate our engagement, and I knew not on what spot I should put my lips..."		Fiction/Classics Pages 240
☐	**The Art of Cross-Examination** by *Francis L. Wellman*	ISBN: 1-59462-309-0	$26.95
	Written by a renowned trial lawyer, Wellman imparts his experience and uses case studies to explain how to use psychology to extract desired information through questioning.		How-to/Science/Reference Pages 408
☐	**Answered or Unanswered?** by *Louisa Vaughan*	ISBN: 1-59462-248-5	$10.95
	Miracles of Faith in China		Religion Pages 112
☐	**The Edinburgh Lectures on Mental Science (1909)** by *Thomas*	ISBN: 1-59462-008-3	$11.95
	This book contains the substance of a course of lectures recently given by the writer in the Queen Street Hail, Edinburgh. Its purpose is to indicate the Natural Principles governing the relation between Mental Action and Material Conditions...		New Age/Psychology Pages 148
☐	**Ayesha** by *H. Rider Haggard*	ISBN: 1-59462-301-5	$24.95
	Verily and indeed it is the unexpected that happens! Probably if there was one person upon the earth from whom the Editor of this, and of a certain previous history, did not expect to hear again...		Classics Pages 380
☐	**Ayala's Angel** by *Anthony Trollope*	ISBN: 1-59462-352-X	$29.95
	The two girls were both pretty, but Lucy who was twenty-one who supposed to be simple and comparatively unattractive, whereas Ayala was credited, as her Bombwhat romantic name might show, with poetic charm and a taste for romance. Ayala when her father died was nineteen...		Fiction Pages 484
☐	**The American Commonwealth** by *James Bryce*	ISBN: 1-59462-286-8	$34.45
	An interpretation of American democratic political theory. It examines political mechanics and society from the perspective of Scotsman James Bryce.		Politics Pages 572
☐	**Stories of the Pilgrims** by *Margaret P. Pumphrey*	ISBN: 1-59462-116-0	$17.95
	This book explores pilgrims religious oppression in England as well as their escape to Holland and eventual crossing to America on the Mayflower, and their early days in New England...		History Pages 268

www.bookjungle.com *email:* sales@bookjungle.com *fax:* 630-214-0564 *mail:* Book Jungle PO Box 2226 Champaign, IL 61825

			QTY
The Fasting Cure by *Sinclair Upton*	ISBN: *1-59462-222-1*	**$13.95**	☐
In the Cosmopolitan Magazine for May, 1910, and in the Contemporary Review (London) for April, 1910, I published an article dealing with my experiences in fasting. I have written a great many magazine articles, but never one which attracted so much attention...		New Age/Self Help/Health Pages 164	
Hebrew Astrology by *Sepharial*	ISBN: *1-59462-308-2*	**$13.45**	☐
In these days of advanced thinking it is a matter of common observation that we have left many of the old landmarks behind and that we are now pressing forward to greater heights and to a wider horizon than that which represented the mind-content of our progenitors...		Astrology Pages 144	
Thought Vibration or The Law of Attraction in the Thought World	ISBN: *1-59462-127-6*	**$12.95**	☐
by *William Walker Atkinson*		Psychology/Religion Pages 144	
Optimism by *Helen Keller*	ISBN: *1-59462-108-X*	**$15.95**	☐
Helen Keller was blind, deaf, and mute since 19 months old, yet famously learned how to overcome these handicaps, communicate with the world, and spread her lectures promoting optimism. An inspiring read for everyone...		Biographies/Inspirational Pages 84	
Sara Crewe by *Frances Burnett*	ISBN: *1-59462-360-0*	**$9.45**	☐
In the first place, Miss Minchin lived in London. Her home was a large, dull, tall one, in a large, dull square, where all the houses were alike, and all the sparrows were alike, and where all the door-knockers made the same heavy sound...		Childrens/Classic Pages 88	
The Autobiography of Benjamin Franklin by *Benjamin Franklin*	ISBN: *1-59462-135-7*	**$24.95**	☐
The Autobiography of Benjamin Franklin has probably been more extensively read than any other American historical work, and no other book of its kind has had such ups and downs of fortune. Franklin lived for many years in England, where he was agent...		Biographies/History Pages 332	

Name	
Email	
Telephone	
Address	
City, State ZIP	

☐ Credit Card   ☐ Check / Money Order

Credit Card Number	
Expiration Date	
Signature	

Please Mail to: Book Jungle
PO Box 2226
Champaign, IL 61825
or Fax to: 630-214-0564

ORDERING INFORMATION

web: *www.bookjungle.com*
email: *sales@bookjungle.com*
fax: *630-214-0564*
mail: *Book Jungle PO Box 2226 Champaign, IL 61825*
or PayPal *to sales@bookjungle.com*

Please contact us for bulk discounts

DIRECT-ORDER TERMS

20% Discount if You Order Two or More Books
Free Domestic Shipping!
Accepted: Master Card, Visa, Discover, American Express

www.ingramcontent.com/pod-product-compliance
Lightning Source LLC
Chambersburg PA
CBHW081328040426
42453CB00013B/2331